Macbeth

for Senior Students

A Dagger of the Mind

Brenda Pinder
With additional material by John Hughes

THE SHAKESPEARE WORKSHOP SERIES
General Editor: Peter Jones

A Midsummer Night's Dream: The Course of True Love – Mark McFadden
Antony and Cleopatra: Gaze on Cleopatra – Wendy Michaels
As You Like It: Love's Keen Arrows – Dennis Robinson and Ken Watson
Hamlet: A Workshop Approach – Brenda Pinder & Ken Watson
Henry IV, Part 1: The Theme of Honour's Tongue – Wendy Michaels
Henry V: We Happy Few – Jo-Anne Nibbs
Julius Caesar: The Dogs of War – Wendy Michaels & Ken Watson
King Lear: Sharper Than A Serpent's Tooth – Brenda Pinder
Macbeth: Creative Work Ideas – Mike Hayhoe
Macbeth for Senior Students: A Dagger of the Mind – Brenda Pinder
Measure for Measure: Some By Virtue Fall – Wayne Sawyer
Much Ado About Nothing: A Skirmish of Wit – Gregory Seach
Othello: The Green Ey'd Monster – Ken Watson & Stuart Wilson
Richard II and *The Winter's Tale: Bitter Bread* – C Radcliffe, D Nicholson & K Watson
Richard III: To Prove A Villain – Calvin Durrant
Romeo and Juliet: Star-Cross'd Lovers – Gordon Shrubb & Ken Watson
The Merchant of Venice: Let Him Look to His Bond – Gregory Seach
The Merry Wives of Windsor: Moonshine Revellers – M Kindler & A Lasaitis
The Taming of the Shrew: Such A Mad Marriage – Ken Watson
The Tempest: Full Fathom Five – Brenda Pinder
Twelfth Night: The Food of Love – Ken Watson

ISBN 0 949898 52 X

St Clair Press

Macbeth for Senior Students: A Dagger of the Mind is published by St Clair Press
an imprint of PHOENIX EDUCATION PTY LTD

Sydney
PO Box 3141, Putney 2112
Tel: (02) 9809 3579 Fax: (02) 9808 1430

Melbourne
PO Box 197, Albert Park 3206
Tel: (03) 9699 8377 Fax: (03) 9699 9242

Email: service@phoenixeduc.com
Website: www.phoenixeduc.com

Printing:
Printed in Australia by Five Senses Education, Seven Hills

Mr. WILLIAM

SHAKESPEARES

COMEDIES, HISTORIES, & TRAGEDIES.

Publiſhed according to the True Originall Copies.

Martius Droeshout sculpsit London

LONDON

Printed by Iſaac Iaggard, and Ed. Blount. 1623.

THE TRAGEDIE OF MACBETH.

Actus Primus. Scœna Prima.

Thunder and Lightning. Enter three Witches.

1\. When shall we three meet againe?
In Thunder, Lightning, or in Raine?
2\. When the Hurley-burley's done,
When the Battaile's lost, and wonne.
3\. That will be ere the set of Sunne.
1\. Where the place?
2\. Vpon the Heath.
3\. There to meet with *Macbeth*.
1\. I come, *Gray-Malkin*.
All. *Padock* calls anon: faire is foule, and foule is faire,
Houer through the fogge and filthie ayre. *Exeunt.*

Scena Secunda.

Alarum within. Enter King Malcome, Donalbaine, Lenox, with attendants, meeting a bleeding Captaine.

King. What bloody man is that? he can report,
As seemeth by his plight, of the Reuolt
The newest state.
Mal. This is the Serieant,
Who like a good and hardie Souldier fought
'Gainst my Captiuitie: Haile braue friend;
Say to the King, the knowledge of the Broyle,
As thou didst leaue it.
Cap. Doubtfull it stood,
As two spent Swimmers, that doe cling together,
And choake their Art: The mercilesse *Macdonwald*
(Worthie to be a Rebell, for to that
The multiplying Villanies of Nature
Doe swarme vpon him) from the Westerne Isles
Of Kernes and Gallowgrosses is supply'd,
And Fortune on his damned Quarry smiling,
Shew'd like a Rebells Whore: but all's too weake:
For braue *Macbeth* (well hee deserues that Name)
Disdayning Fortune, with his brandisht Steele,
Which smoak'd with bloody execution
(Like Valours Minion) caru'd out his passage,
Till hee fac'd the Slaue:
Which neu'r shooke hands, nor bad farwell to him,
Till he vnseam'd him from the Naue toth' Chops,
And fix'd his Head vpon our Battlements.
King. O valiant Cousin, worthy Gentleman.
Cap. As whence the Sunne 'gins his reflection,
Shipwracking Stormes, and direfull Thunders:
So from that Spring, whence comfort seem'd to come,
Discomfort swells: Marke King of Scotland, marke,
No sooner Iustice had, with Valour arm'd,
Compell'd these skipping Kernes to trust their heeles,
But the Norweyan Lord, surueying vantage,
With furbusht Armes, and new supplyes of men,
Began a fresh assault.
King. Dismay'd not this our Captaines, *Macbeth* and *Banquoh*?
Cap. Yes, as Sparrowes, Eagles;
Or the Hare, the Lyon:
If I say sooth, I must report they were
As Cannons ouer-charg'd with double Cracks,
So they doubly redoubled stroakes vpon the Foe:
Except they meant to bathe in reeking Wounds,
Or memorize another *Golgotha*,
I cannot tell: but I am faint,
My Gashes cry for helpe.
King. So well thy words become thee, as thy wounds,
They smack of Honor both: Goe get him Surgeons.

Enter Rosse and Angus.

Who comes here?
Mal. The worthy *Thane* of Rosse.
Lenox. What a haste lookes through his eyes?
So should he looke, that seemes to speake things strange.
Rosse. God saue the King.
King. Whence cam'st thou, worthy *Thane*?
Rosse. From Fiffe, great King,
Where the Norweyan Banners flowt the Skie,
And fanne our people cold.
Norway himselfe, with terrible numbers,
Assisted by that most disloyall Traytor,
The *Thane* of Cawdor, began a dismall Conflict,
Till that *Bellona's* Bridegroome, lapt in proofe,
Confronted him with selfe-comparisons,
Point against Point, rebellious Arme 'gainst Arme,
Curbing his lauish spirit: and to conclude,
The Victorie fell on vs.
King. Great happinesse.
Rosse. That now *Sweno*, the Norwayes King,
Craues composition:
Nor would we deigne him buriall of his men,
Till he disbursed, at Saint *Colmes* ynch,
Ten thousand Dollars, to our generall vse.

King. No

◆ Contents ◆

The activities in this book have been prepared for senior students.

While the earlier St Clair publication, *Creative Work Ideas for Macbeth* contains some activities suitable for senior students, it was prepared with mainly younger students in mind.

Parallels

◆ Evidence ◆

1. An ambitious businessman, egged on by his wife, moves to displace the Chairman of the company from the Board by discrediting him. He goes on to remove all opposition by inventing scandals about anyone who stands in his way.

   Improvise a conversation between him and his wife at any point in their scheming.

2. The 'Godfather' of a gangster group is secretly murdered by his right-hand man, who is encouraged by his wife.

   Improvise a conversation by two other members of the gang about their suspicions of murder.

3. The victim of a murderer turns up as a ghost at a dinner party at the murderer's house.

   Improvise the situation in which the murderer sees the ghost but no one else does.

◆ Activity ◆

These three brief outlines represent parallels to certain aspects of *Macbeth*. Start by working in pairs or fours to devise and rehearse one of these improvisations.

Keep it short and try to bring out any parallels you can with the corresponding situation in *Macbeth*.

Next, in the same groups, invent your own parallel about any aspect of the play. Don't try to mirror too much of *Macbeth*; just take *one* incident or a small section of dialogue as your starting point or model. For example: Lady Macduff believing her husband has deserted his family when he has really gone to seek help. You should set your improvisation in any period you like—it doesn't *have* to be in modern times.

◆ Follow up ◆

Macbeth Update:
Work in groups of about four or five and transpose one of Macbeth's crimes (Duncan, Banquo, or the slaughter of Macduff's wife and children) into modern times and imagine how it would be presented by the media.

You could choose to present newspaper extracts (perhaps from both tabloids and 'quality' newspapers) which give the official account but which hint at other explanations. Alternatively, you could devise a television newscast, or an interview with an 'insider' about the mysterious death. Whatever medium you choose, try to convey not only the 'official' story but also hints of suspicions, carefully restrained or implied because of fear of reprisals.

An example might be an interview with Macduff about what happened at Glamis the night of Duncan's murder. (Look at Act 2, scene 4 to see some hints of his suspicions.)

When groups share their work with the rest of the class, through performance and/or display, discuss what light is shed by each group on the play.

Opening Scene

◆ Evidence ◆

Thunder and lightning. Enter three WITCHES.

First Witch	When shall we three meet again In thunder, lightning, or in rain?
Second Witch	When the hurlyburly's done, When the battle's lost and won.
Third Witch	That will be ere the set of sun.
First Witch	Where the place?
Second Witch	Upon the heath.
Third Witch	There to meet with Macbeth.
First Witch	I come Greymalkin!
Second Witch	Paddock calls.
Third Witch	Anon!
All	Fair is foul, and foul is fair; Hover through the fog and filthy air.

◆ Activity ◆

This is one of the most arresting and dramatic openings of any play. The rhythms of the witches' speeches are quite different from Shakespeare's usual blank verse and the use of rhyme creates an effect of an incantation or spell. The calls to their 'familiars'—Greymalkin (grey cat) and Paddock (toad) reinforce this feeling.

The language also has a sense of paradox: 'When the battle's lost and won' and 'Fair is foul and foul is fair'. There is an immediate sense of deceptive double meaning, of possibly dangerous ambiguity. It is hard not to sense an atmosphere of evil.

Working in groups of three, read the scene several times and work out ways of creating an atmosphere of foreboding, menace and potential evil.

In Shakespeare's theatre, when performances were normally in broad daylight, with many of the audience in the open air (see drawing of the Globe Theatre below), there was a need to have openings that arrested the attention of the audience. As there few technical resources compared with a modern theatre, language was critical. Compare this to a modern production that relies on dimming the house lights and on a wide range of visual and sound effects.

Staying in threes, imagine that you are **not** limited to words alone and that you are making a film of the play with great possibilities for settings and effects. The Roman Polanski film starts with a bleak sea shore and three lonely ragged figures on the skyline, but there are an infinite number of ways to begin. Discuss the possibilities and choose a sequence of camera shots with which to start your film **before** any words are spoken. Write each shot on a separate line, somewhat like this:

1. Opening shot of sky with ominous gusting clouds
2. Camera moves down to battlefield; scattered bodies; torn pennant flapping
3. Three figures outlined against sky, picking over the bodies for valuables

and so on, for about ten shots.

The next stage is to expand your descriptions a little further, pinpointing exactly what picture you want to capture. Then go through the descriptions, removing all the instructions and references to cameras and shots. What you will have left is a series of images, each on a separate line — making a poem. Re-arrange lines as you wish, polish where necessary, and then make a clean copy for display.

◆ Follow up ◆

While this opening is in your mind, think about the essential nature of a play and how it differs from a novel. How might the novel *Macbeth* begin? It would have greater flexibility in playing around with time — the whole story could perhaps be told in flashback. Or it could be in the first person, with one of the participants alive at the end recording his version of events. In a third person narrative, the author could reveal the thoughts of any or all of the characters, and could comment on events him/herself.

Try your hand at a few paragraphs of the novel of *Macbeth*, giving a slightly different slant on events from that of the play, and bringing out any differences you can in narrative style and form.

Group Performance

◆ Evidence ◆

Thunder. Enter the three WITCHES

First Witch	Thrice the brinded cat hath mew'd
Second Witch	Thrice and once the hedge-pig whin'd /
Third Witch	Harpier cries "Tis time, 'Tis time" /
First Witch	Round about the cauldron go;
	In the poison'd entrails throw /
	Toad, that under cold stone
	Days and nights hast thirty-one /
	Swelter'd venom sleeping got,
	Boil thou first i' th' charmed pot./
All	Double, double toil and trouble;
	Fire burn, and cauldron bubble /
Second Witch	Fillet of a fenny snake,
	In the cauldron boil and bake /
	Eye of newt, and toe of frog
	Wool of bat, and tongue of dog /
	Adder's fork and blind-worm's sting
	Lizard's leg , and howlet's wing /
	For a charm of powerful trouble
	Like a hell-broth boil and bubble. /
All	Double, double toil and trouble;
	Fire burn, and cauldron bubble. /
Third Witch	Scale of dragon, tooth of wolf,
	Witches' mummy / maw and gulf
	Of the ravin'd salt-sea shark /
	Root of hemlock digg'd i' the dark, /
	Liver of blaspheming Jew /
	Gall of goat, and slips of yew
	Sliver'd in the moon's eclipse /
	Nose of Turk, and Tartar's lips /
	Finger of birth-strangled babe
	Ditch-deliver'd by a drab /
	Make the gruel thick and slab /
	Add thereto a tiger's chaudron,
	For th' ingredients of our cauldron /
All	Double, double toil and trouble;
	Fire burn and cauldron bubble /
Second Witch	Cool it with a baboon's blood /
	Then the charm is firm and good. /

◆ Activity ◆

You will need a good sized space for this as you will be creating a performance of the witches' spell-making.

Divide the lines of the scene amongst you. (The marks in the lines above suggest possible break points, but you should choose your own if you wish to.) Write your line or lines on a card. Then number all the cards in the order in which they come in the scene, so you can learn your cues.

Now split up to learn your line(s). Walk about saying it to yourself in lots of different ways—shouting, whispering, with anxiety, with sinister meaning, and so on. Finally, settle on one way of delivering it which is your own. Run through all the lines in the right order to get the cues clear and learn whose line you follow.

As a group, decide on a way of setting the scene. You could have an imaginary cauldron in the centre and start from the edges of the room, moving in to drop your 'ingredient' into the cauldron on your line. You might then wish to form a sort of tableau of kneeling and crouching figures, gradually built up as more lines are spoken and more actors are added to the scene. Or you might like to use your bodies to create a sinister moving mass, filling the stage; or witches could circle the cauldron throughout the speaking of the lines.

Use your ingenuity to devise imaginative ways to experiment with the scene, then settle on one approach for your performance. You will be creating a theatrical experience for the participants that will give far more insight into the power of the words than a reading could possibly do.

◆ Follow up ◆

Work in groups of about six for this activity. From the play find a series of lines spoken by the Witches and their spirits to Macbeth. Look at the greetings in Act 1, scene 2, some of the lines of the apparitions from Act 4, scene 1, and a few other lines that seem to you to embody the message of the witches, such as 'Fair is foul and foul is fair' or 'Show his eyes and grieve his heart'. You need to collect about ten or twelve scraps of text to be shared amongst all members of the group, except one. This person is to be Macbeth and he/she stands in the middle while the others circle around whispering their temptations in his ear, or perhaps turning him physically to each of them to receive each line. Use your imagination to create your own script from your chosen lines and to make it into a dramatic performance.

Show your scene to the rest of the class and ask each of the Macbeths to tell you what it felt like to be at the centre of this threatening circle.

Missing Words

◆ Evidence ◆

To be thus is nothing,
but to be .... thus: our fears in Banquo 1
Stick deep, and in his .... of nature 2
Reigns that which would be fear'd; 'tis much he dares;
And, to that dauntless temper of his 3
He hath a wisdom that doth guide his valour
To act in safety. There is .... but he 4
Whose being I do fear; and under him
My Genius is rebuk'd; as, it is said,
Mark Anthony's was by .... He chid the Sisters, 5
When first they put the name of .... upon me, 6
And bade them speak to him; then, prophet-like,
They .... him father to a line of kings: 7
Upon my head they plac'd a .... crown, 8
And put a barren sceptre in my gripe,
Thence to be wrench'd with an unlineal hand,
No son of mine succeeding. If't be so,
For .... issue have I fil'd my mind; 9
For them the gracious Duncan have I 10
Put rancours in the vessel of my peace,
Only for them; and mine eternal ....
Given to the common Enemy of man,
To make them kings, the .... of Banquo kings! 12
Rather than so, come, fate, into the list,
And champion me to th' utterance!—Who's there?—

◆ Activity ◆

This is the soliloquy in which Macbeth reveals to the audience his fears about Banquo and prepares us for the interview with the Murderers which follows. Some of the words in the speech have been omitted. Work in pairs to see if you can guess what might fit in the spaces. There are a number of clues that might help:

- when read aloud, the blank verse rhythm will usually suggest how many syllables there are in the missing word;
- the syntax will show whether it is a noun, verb, adjective or adverb;
- the feelings of Macbeth should provide clues about the words he might use.

When you have your suggestions about the missing words, look at the original in Act 3, scene 1 and compare it with your version. It's not an issue of being 'right' or 'wrong'. You may even come up with some suggestions that **you** think are better than the original. The value of this exercise is in the close focus on language that it involves.

◆ Follow up ◆

In the same pairs, try this **sequencing** puzzle.

The words below are out-of-order sections of a speech by Lady Macbeth when she is reproaching Macbeth for cowardly behaviour at the feast. See if you can sort them into the right order.

This is the air-drawn dagger which, you said,
Led you to Duncan

Authoris'd by her grandam

Shame itself!
Why do you make such faces

O proper stuff!
This is the very painting of your fear.

When all's done,
You look but on a stool.

O, these flaws and starts
(Impostors to true fear) would well become
A woman's story at a winter's fire.

After deciding on a sequence, deliver the speech in the order you have chosen. Compare your version with the original. (See Act 3, scene 4)

Sources

◆ Evidence ◆

And suerlie herevpon had he put Makduffe to death, but that certaine witch, who hee had in great trust, had told that he should neuer be slaine with man borne of anie woman, nor vanquished till the wood of Bernane came to the castell of Dunsinane. By the prophesie Makbeth put all feare out of his heart, supposing he might doo what he would, without anie fear feare to be punished for the same, for by the one prophesie he beleeued it was vnpossible for anie man to vanquish him, and by the other vnpossible to slea him. This vain hope caused him to doo manie outragious things, to the greeuous oppression of his subjects.

At length therefore, communicating his purposed intent with his trustie friends, amongst whome Banquo was the chiefest, vpon confidence of their promised aid, he slue the king at Enuerns, or (as some say) at Botgosuane, in the sixt yeare of his reigne

◆ Activity ◆

These are two passages from an Elizabethan historian called **Holinshed**, whose work Shakespeare used as a source for the story of *Macbeth*. He used parts of two separate accounts, combining two different kings in his character Macbeth: **Donwald**, who, egged on by his wife, slew King Duff, who was a guest in his castle at the time, and put the blame on his drunken chamberlains, and **Makbeth**, who murdered King Duncan, a weak king whose rule was so slack that it brought on outbreaks of violence and sedition.

Look at the two extracts above from Holinshed. You can see that the basis of the witches and apparitions came directly from this account, but there is also a considerable difference in Shakespeare's handling of the King's murder. In Holinshed, Makbeth does not act alone but with 'trustie friends amongst whom Banquo was the chiefest'.

- With a partner, explore reasons Shakespeare may have had for changing this. What might he have wanted to emphasise?

- The sleepwalking scene has no basis in Holinshed, nor does the appearance of Banquo's ghost at the banquet. How do you think each of these additions affects the play?

Make some brief notes on your thoughts and use them in a class discussion on what we learn about Shakespeare's intentions from the changes he has made to his sources.

◆ Follow up ◆

Shakespeare's Banquo

In Holinshed, Banquo is Macbeth's accomplice. In Shakespeare's play, he is certainly not an accomplice, but is he entirely without blame? For example, look at the scene where he and Macbeth are greeted by the witches (Act 1, scene 3). How does Banquo react to the promises about his heirs?

He seems to be warning Macbeth not to be tempted by the 'truths' told by the witches, and this strikes us as the voice of sanity when contrasted with Macbeth's 'fantastical' thoughts of murder.

Look also at his brief appearance in Act 2, scene 1 when he tells his son of his fear of sleep and the 'cursed thoughts' it may produce. He then introduces the subject of the 'three weird sisters' into his conversation with Macbeth. It seems likely that he would put two and two together when Duncan dies so suspiciously. He makes his suspicions clear in his soliloquy at the opening of Act 3—yet he does not speak out. Why?

- Discuss Banquo's motives (fear? ambition? loyalty to a friend? etc.) and then make your own notes to prepare for an essay on this topic:

  What is the dramatic importance of Banquo in the play?

Two-Handed Soliloquy

◆ Evidence ◆

Macbeth If it were done, when 'tis done, then 'twere well
It were done quickly; if th' assassination
Could trammel up the consequence, and catch,
With his surcease, success; that but this blow
Might be the be-all and the end-all—here,
But here, upon this bank and shoal of time,
We'd jump the life to come. But in these cases,
We still have judgement here; that we but teach
Bloody instructions, which being taught, return
To plague the inventor; this even-handed justice
Commends th' ingredients of our poison'd chalice
To our own lips. He's here in double trust:
First, as I am his kinsman and his subject,
Strong both against the deed; then, as his host,
Who should against his murderer shut the door,
Not bear the knife myself. Besides, this Duncan
Hath borne his faculties so meek, hath been
So clear in his great office, that his virtues
Will plead like angels, trumpet-tongu'd, against
The deep damnation of his taking-off;
And pity, like a naked new-born babe,
Striding the blast, or heaven's cherubin, hors'd
Upon the sightless couriers of the air,
Shall blow the horrid deed in every eye,
That tears shall drown the wind. I have no spur
To prick the sides of my intent, but only
Vaulting ambition, which o'er-leaps itself
And falls on the other.

(Act1, scene 7)

◆ Activity ◆

Working in pairs, read the speech, taking alternate 'sense units'—that is, sections which are complete ideas, usually marked off by full stops, semi-colons or conjunctions like 'and' or 'but'.

Now turn the speech into a dialogue between the two halves of Macbeth's mind, the part that feels loyalty to his king and guest, and the part determined to seize the crown by any means thought necessary. Each person in the pair is to take one of these two 'voices'. Try to think of ways of presenting these conflicting voices in action.

For example, one person could be sitting in a chair while the other circles around, tempting and whispering into first one ear and then the other. Or you could sit back to back—presenting the two faces of the one man—or facing one another, profile to profile. Whatever you choose, the aim is to show Macbeth's dilemma dramatically.

What conclusions does Macbeth come to after these deliberations? How is his mind changed again later in the scene?

◆ Follow up ◆

In pairs, select about four or five lines of Lady Macbeth in the rest of the scene that seem to you to show her powers of persuasion. Share your lines with the rest of the class and discuss why they show Lady Macbeth's persuasiveness.

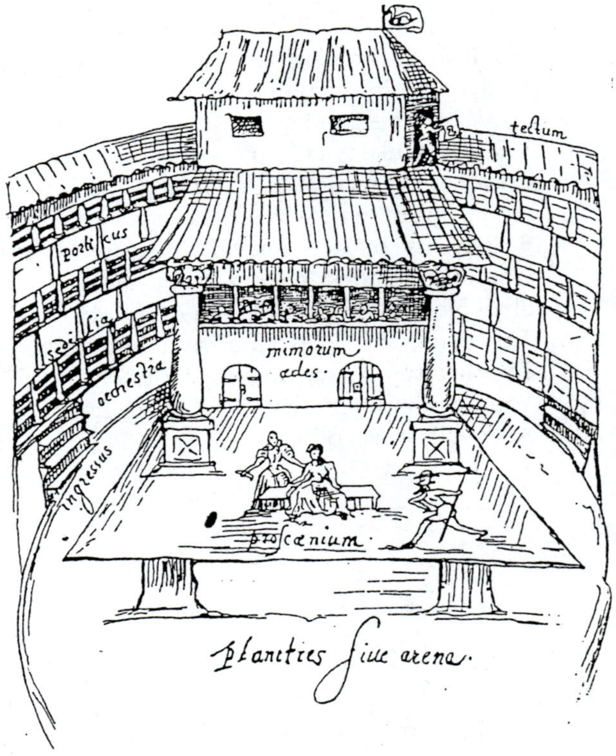

The Porter

◆ Evidence ◆

Porter Here's a knocking indeed! If a man were porter of hell-gate, he should have old turning the key. [*Knock*] Knock, knock, knock! Who's there, i' th' name of Beelzebub! Here's a farmer that hang'd himself on the expectation of plenty. Come in time; have napkins enow about you; here you'll sweat for't. [*Knock*] Knock, knock! Who's there i' th' other devil's name! Faith, here's an equivocator, that could swear in both the scales against either scale; who committed treason enough for God's sake, yet could not equivocate to heaven. O, come in, equivocator. *Knock*] Knock, knock! Who's there? Faith, here's an English tailor come hither for stealing out of a French hose. Come in, tailor, here you may roast your goose. [*Knock*] Knock, knock, never at quiet! What are you? But this place is too cold for hell. I'll devil-porter it no further. I had thought to have let in some of all professions that go the primrose way to th' everlasting bonfire. [*Knock*] Anon, anon! [*Opens the gate*] I pray you remember the porter.

It's hard for a modern production to succeed completely with this scene. Many of the Porter's lines contain contemporary references that audiences of Shakespeare's time would have picked up easily (and some of which help to date the play fairly precisely). Shakespeare's audience would have laughed readily at the references, but these are mostly lost on an audience today.

For example, take the references to an 'equivocator'. It is likely that the 'equivocator' was a Father Garnet, a Jesuit priest who was tried and executed for his part in the Guy Fawkes plot. His alias was 'Farmer', so another reference to him is probably intended in the fourth line.

The notes in any edition will give you more explanations of other obscure lines, but they don't help us very much in understanding the dramatic effect of the scene. The Porter was to the contemporary audience what a modern satirical comedian is today, commenting on politicians, terrorists or the Royal Family, or anyone else in the news.

Look at the theme of 'Porter of Hell-gate'. The fact that we have just witnessed the murder of a king by his subject and host makes the Porter's 'role' take on a strong sense of irony. He is, in a real sense, gatekeeper to a kind of Hell, though he is unaware of it. The effect of this irony is sometimes referred to as 'comic relief', but, despite the laughter, it is an **increase in tension** (rather than relief from tension) that audiences usually experience as they wait for the inevitable discovery of Duncan's murder.

◆ Activity ◆

Working in pairs, try to rewrite the Porter's first speech in modern terms. Keep the idea of his being Porter of Hell but replace his contemporary references with modern equivalents. Choose your candidates for Hell from people or professions in the news now.

For example:

> 'O come in, Politician! Here your broken promises are waiting for you!
> Your Public Relations men are here before you! ...

or

> 'Who's there? A terrorist blown up by his own bomb? ...

Rehearse your new version of the speech and present it to the rest of the class.

◆ Follow up ◆

Read the rest of the Porter's scene aloud in pairs and plan how you would stage it as part of a production of the whole play. How will you dress the Porter? How is he to show he is drunk? How will you bring out the vulgarity of much of what he says? (See especially his references to lechery and urine.)

Make a **prompt copy** of the scene by photocopying a section of the text and pasting it in the centre of a large sheet of paper. Use the space around it to mark actors' moves and directions for lighting and sound cues for your Stage Manager. Add a plan for the set with moves marked on it, and Director's notes for the actor who is to play the Porter, incorporating the ideas you have discussed. Share all this work between the two of you and display your finished results for all to see.

Alter Ego

◆ Evidence ◆

This dialogue is between Macbeth and Banquo near the beginning of Act 3, scene 1.

Macbeth Tonight we hold a solemn supper, sir,
And I'll request your presence.
Banquo Let your Highness
Command upon me; to the which my duties
Are with a most indissoluble tie
For ever knit.
Macbeth Ride you this afternoon?
Banquo: Ay, my good lord.
Macbeth We should have else desir'd your good advice—
Which still hath been both grave and prosperous—
In this day's council; but we'll take tomorrow.
Is't far you ride?
Banquo As far, my lord, as will fill up the time
'Twixt this and supper; go not my horse the better,
I must become a borrower of the night
For a dark hour or twain.
Macbeth Fail not our feast.
Banquo My lord, I will not.
Macbeth We hear our bloody cousins are bestow'd
In England and in Ireland, not confessing
Their cruel parricide, filling their hearers
With strange invention; but of that tomorrow,
When, therewithal, we shall have cause of state
Craving us jointly. Hie you to horse; adieu,
'Till you return at night. Goes Fleance with you?
Banquo Ay, my good lord: our time does call upon's.
Macbeth I wish your horses swift and sure of foot;
And so I do commend you to their backs.
Farewell. [*Exit Banquo*]

◆ Activity ◆

As a class, discuss briefly what you think is going on in the minds of these two characters as they talk. Macbeth clearly wants to find out where Banquo is riding and when he will return to the castle. Why? What does Banquo make of all these questions? Is he suspicious? (Notice his soliloquy that begins this scene.)

Divide into fours for the next step. Two people speak the lines of the dialogue as they are written and the other two are to be the 'alter egos' of Macbeth and Banquo. The alter egos speak the characters' innermost, secret thoughts. The whole scene will have to be scripted by the four people, as you jointly decide when the 'thought speeches' are to be inserted, as well as what is to be said.

Rehearse the scene either as a radio play (which you could tape) or as a staged reading with actions added in. Present your complete scene to the rest of the class and compare the additions each group has made to the original dialogue.

◆ Follow up ◆

Two volunteers read the dialogue between Macbeth and Lady Macbeth in Act 1, scene 7, line 29 to end of scene. The class then divides into two groups, one to sit behind Macbeth, the other behind Lady Macbeth. These two groups are the thoughts of the respective characters and they utter what they think is in the minds of the character, in pauses between the scripted lines. The two actors in the centre have to decide at what points they will pause for the thoughts to well up. You will probably need more than one go at this activity as the 'thoughts' may not come easily at first. When everyone gains confidence, the activity can be very valuable. It's important to **listen** to the lines rather than follow them in a text so that you respond spontaneously to what is said.

Afterwards, discuss briefly what seemed most apt and appropriate amongst the thoughts expressed.

Bystanders

◆ Evidence ◆

Lennox May it please your Highness sit?

The Ghost of Banquo *enters, and sits in* Macbeth's *place.*

Macbeth Here had we now our country's honour roof'd,
Were the grac'd person of our Banquo present;
Who I may rather challenge for unkindness,
Than pity for mischance!
Ross His absence, sir,
Lays blame upon his promise. Please 't your highness
To grace us with your royal company?
Macbeth The Table's full.
Lennox Here is a place reserv'd, sir.
Macbeth Where?
Lennox Here, my good lord. What is 't that moves your highness?
Macbeth' Which of you have done this?
Lords What, my good lord?
Macbeth Thou canst not say I did it: never shake
Thy gory locks at me.
Ross Gentlemen, rise; his highness is not well.
Lady Macbeth Sit, worthy friends: my lord is often thus,
And hath been from his youth: pry you, keep seat;
The fit is momentary; upon a thought
He will again be well. If much you note him,
You shall offend him and extend his passion:
Feed, and regard him not. [*Aside to Macbeth*] Are you a man?
Macbeth Ay, and a bold one, that dare look on that
Which might appal the devil.

◆ Activity ◆

This is part of Act 3, scene 4, the scene in which the ghost of Banquo appears to Macbeth, though no one else sees it.

If you look at the stage directions at the beginning of the scene, you will see that not only are certain 'named' characters present at this scene, but also 'Lords and Attendants'.

Imagine that you are one of these—either a Lord who has been commanded to attend this celebration, or an Attendant who perhaps waits at the table or serves wine. You obviously don't see the ghost and probably don't hear any of Macbeth's conversation with the Murderers' at the door, but surely you would notice his strange behaviour?

In pairs, create a short dialogue in which your character returns home and is questioned by his/her wife/husband (or friend) about the events at the banquet. Then swap parts and let the other person have a turn at the reporting. Then choose **one** of these two scenes to rehearse and to share with another pair.

◆ Follow up ◆

- Use the ideas that have emerged from the activity above to make up a letter or diary entry for the character you chose.
- Then choose another incident in the play where a character's thoughts are not revealed to us by soliloquy and write your own 'stream of thoughts' to show what is going through his/her mind. Use punctuation only in order to create the impression of ideas running through the mind—dashes and rows of dots can be particularly useful.

Some possibilities include:

- Lady Macbeth greeting Duncan as he arrives at Glamis castle. (Act 1, scene 6)
- Malcolm or Donalbain hearing news of their father's death. (Act 2, scene 3)
- Malcolm testing Macduff's loyalty. (Act 4, scene 3)
- Macduff resolving to revenge the murder of his wife and children. (Act 4, scene 3)

Alternative Viewpoint : Malcolm

◆ Evidence ◆

Malcolm We shall not spend a large expense of time,
Before we reckon with your several loves,
And make us even with you. My thanes and kinsmen,
Henceforth be earls, the first that ever Scotland
In such an honour nam'd. What's more to do,
Which would be planted newly with the time—
As calling home our exil'd friends abroad
That fled the snares of watchful tyranny;
Producing forth the cruel ministers
Of this dead butcher and his fiend-like queen,
Who, as 'tis thought, by self and violent hands
Took off her life—this, and what needful else
That calls upon us, by the grace of Grace,
We will perform in measure, time, and place.
So, thanks to all at once, and to each one,
Whom we invite to see us crown'd at Scone. (Act 5, scene 7)

Malcolm promises in this last speech of the play to reward his loyal supporters and put right all of Macbeth's wrongs, thus re-establishing justice in the kingdom. There is hope for Scotland again.

◆ Activity ◆

What do you think Malcolm would remember as he looked back over the events of the play? He is present in Act 1, scene 2 when news of the bravery of Macbeth and Banquo reaches his father and he is there, too, when Duncan thanks and rewards them and he is named as heir (Act 1, scene 4). The next time we meet him is on arrival with the king's party at Glamis (Act 1, scene 6), when he says nothing. Then there's the discovery of his father's murder in Act 2, scene 3, and his decision to leave for England.

Work individually on this activity. Think yourself into Malcolm's viewpoint, then write his account — in letters or a diary — of the events he witnesses as well as his own record of his time in England and his testing of Macduff. Add, too, the defeat of Macbeth and his feelings and resolutions at that time. (You might imagine him inviting his brother's return from Ireland and sending him this account with the invitation.)

Seeing the events from a different point of view will help to anchor them in your memory.

◆ Follow up ◆

Choose any other character in the play and record his/her account of some part of the action in a diary/journal form.

It could be interesting, for example, to explore Lady Macbeth's point of view. After the early scenes we see very little of her thoughts and feelings until the sleepwalking shows us her troubled conscience. You could imagine her gradual sense of estrangement from her husband and her descent into instability and depression. Although you will be inventing material, try to base it on evidence, or at least hints, that can be found in the play.

Kingship

◆ Evidence ◆

Malcolm
I grant him bloody,
Luxurious, avaricious, false, deceitful,
Sudden, malicious, smacking of every sin
That has a name; but there's no bottom, none,
In my voluptuousness: your wives, your daughters,
Your matrons, and your maids, could not fill up
The cistern of my lust, and my desire
All continent impediments would o'erbear
That did oppose my will; better Macbeth
Than such an one to reign.

Macduff
Boundless intemperance
In nature is a tyranny; it hath been
Th' untimely emptying of the unhappy throne,
And fall of many kings. But fear not yet
To take upon you what is yours; you may
Convey your pleasures in a spacious plenty,
And yet seem cold—the time you may so hoodwink.
We have willing dames enough; there cannot be
That vulture in you, to devour so many
As will to greatness dedicate themselves,
Finding it so inclin'd.

Malcolm
With this there grows
In my most ill-compos'd affection such
A staunchless avarice that, were I king,
I should cut off the nobles for their lands,
Desire his jewels and this other's house;
And my more-having would be as a sauce
To make me hunger more, that I should forge
Quarrels unjust against the good and the loyal,
Destroying them for wealth.

Macduff
This avarice
Sticks deeper, grows with more pernicious root
Than summer-seeming lust; and it hath been
The sword of our slain kings: yet do not fear;
Scotland hath foisons to fill up your will,
Of your mere own; all these are portable
With other graces weigh'd.

Malcolm
But I have none: the king-becoming graces,
As justice, verity, temperance, stableness,
Bounty, perseverance, mercy, lowliness,
Devotion, patience, courage, fortitude
I have no relish of them, but abound
In the division of each several crime,
Acting it many ways. Nay, had I power, I should
Pour the sweet milk of concord into hell,
Uproar the universal peace, confound
All unity on earth.

◆ Activity ◆

Malcolm thinks that if Macduff should turn out to be a spy of Macbeth's he will go along with any amount of this pretended self-detraction by Malcolm and make no objection. But eventually Macduff despairs of Scotland's hopes and thus shows himself a loyal subject. It does seem a somewhat elaborate device to test Macduff's loyalty, but behind Malcolm's words lies a structure of Elizabethan thinking about the duties owed to and by a king. It also provides a measure by which the audience can judge Macbeth's rule of Scotland. There aren't many of these 'king-becoming graces' that Macbeth can claim. Can you think of any? Would 'courage' and fortitude' be two?

From the little evidence the play offers, how does Duncan match this picture of the ideal king? He is certainly admired—Macbeth himself speaks of him with extravagant praise when he is weighing up motives for murdering him, as against his obligations as host and protector (Act 1, scene 7), and again when he explains his killing of the grooms (Act 2, scene 3).

Working in pairs, search for evidence of the following kingly qualities in Duncan's behaviour and speech and in what others say about him:

- **Justice** (remember Cawdor)
- **Bounty** (that is, generosity)
- **Lowliness** (humility)

You could add to these his praise of Macbeth and Banquo in Act 1, scene 4, and his gracious arrival at Glamis (Act 1, scene 6).

In spite of his qualities, Duncan has one serious deficiency as a king. He does not see either Cawdor ('There's no art to find the mind's construction in the face') or Macbeth ('It is a peerless kinsman') as they really are. Lack of good judgement of character is quite a deficiency in a ruler.

◆ Individual Activity ◆

Write Duncan's obituary for one of the 'quality' newspapers. It is customary in an obituary to emphasise the good features of the deceased, but you can tactfully hint at faults as well.

◆ Follow up ◆

Work in pairs to develop a television newscast about Malcolm's succession to the throne at the end of the play. One person could be the newsreader and the other someone who knows Malcolm well and has agreed to be interviewed about the sort of king he will make. Try to use the play as the main source of information.

Punctuation for Dramatic Effect

◆ Evidence ◆

Macduff this noble passion
Child of integrity hath from my soul
Wip'd the black scruples reconcil'd my thought
To thy good truth and honour devilish Macbeth
By many of these trains hath sought to win me
Into his power and modest wisdom plucks me
From over credulous haste but god above
Deal between thee and me for even now
I put myself to thy direction and
Unspeak my own detraction here abjure
The taints and blames I laid upon myself
For strangers to my nature I am yet
Unknown to woman never was forsworn
Scarcely have coveted what was mine own
At no time broke my faith would not betray
The devil to his fellow and delight
No less in truth than life my first false speaking
Was this upon myself what I am truly
Is thine and my poor country's to command
Whither indeed before thy here approach
Old Siward with ten thousand warlike men
Already at a point was setting forth
Now we ll together and the chance of goodness
Be like our warranted quarrel

◆ Activity ◆

Much of the punctuation in Shakespeare's plays is the work of modern editors. His own punctuation was largely dramatic in function rather than grammatical.

The passage above has had all of the punctuation removed. The intention of this activity, however, is not to look at textual problems of punctuation, but to develop some insight into the rhythms of the blank verse line and the effects Shakespeare achieves with it.

Read the passage silently to yourself to see if you can make some sense of it. and notice where you think each 'sense unit' ends — usually marked by a full stop, semi-colon or conjunction like 'and' or 'but'. Then sit in a circle and read the speech aloud around the circle, taking one 'sense unit' each in turn. If you think someone is mistaken, say so and try to settle on an agreed change. This may mean having a second or third go at it before you are satisfied. When you come to the end, go round again, but this time read a **whole line** each, and keeping the sense of it going. Don't let your voice drop at the end of a line unless the sense unit finishes there as well. Where necessary, try to pick up the meaning from the person before you in your intonation. Use pauses where they come naturally, at ends of sentences or clauses.

At the same time, **listen** to the two rhythms that are going on simultaneously — the normal speech rhythms of the syntax and the underlying beat of the blank verse. It is the tensions created between the two that makes Shakespeare's verse so flexible — at times indistinguishable from real speech, and at other times rising to lyrical heights.

◆ Follow up ◆

Working in pairs, choose a short passage from the play which has particularly lyrical qualities. For example:

> She should have died hereafter ... (Act 5, scene 5)
> Light thickens and the crow makes wing to the rooky wood ...
> (Act 3, scene 4)

Copy a few lines of your passage and mark it on the strong stresses. Blank verse is a five-beat line, usually of ten syllables, in which the strong and weak syllables tend to alternate.

For example (stressed syllabes are italicised):

> *Ay*, in the *cata*lo*g*ue ye *go* for *men*
>
> As *hounds* and *grey*hounds, *mon*grels, *span*iels, *curs*,
>
> *Shou*ghs, *wa*ter rugs and *demi-wol*ves are *clep*t
>
> *All* by the *name* of *dog*s.

Read your lines aloud in a natural way, not emphasising the stresses, and notice how the underlying rhythms merge into the patterns of ordinary speech.

Image Search

◆ Evidence ◆

Fair is foul and foul is fair.

... function is smother'd in surmise
And nothing is but what is not.

There's no art
To find the mind's construction in the face.

Look like the innocent flower
But be the serpent under 't.

Why do you dress me in borrow'd robes?

False face must hide what the false heart doth know.

And make our faces vizards to our hearts
Disguising what they are.

These statements from the play offer a few examples of imagery, all drawn from the first half of the play. What do you think they have in common?

◆ Activity ◆

You will see that the examples above are all related to false appearances, with hiding evil under innocent-seeming disguises. There are many more examples in the play and, as we watch and listen, they gradually work upon us to modify our views of characters and events, each one coming to us with the accumulated force of the previous occurrences. Recurring imagery therefore has an important influence on the ways in which we experience and interpret the play.

Imagery is the use of imaginative comparisons to create a picture in words. If the comparison is stated it is called a simile; if implied, (as when one thing is identified with the other), it is called a metaphor. In fact, any non-literal use of language amounts to imagery.

Work in five groups. Each group selects **one** Act to skim through, looking for any effective images and grouping them under these headings:

- **Blood**
- **Darkness and Light**
- **Clothes / Robes / Disguises**
- **False Appearances**
- **Others**

Collect and collate the images in your Act, sharing the work amongst members of the group. Record the images on large sheets of paper pinned to a wall and divided into headed sections.

You won't, of course, remember all the quotations in an exam or when writing an essay, but the connected groups of images do help memory as well as providing much evidence of mood, theme and atmosphere in the play.

◆ Follow up ◆

Working individually, decide which of the images collected when working in a group seems to you to best sum up the play. Would it be a 'dagger of the mind' or the wood of Birnam on the move? Or a witches' cauldron of unspeakable ingredients and evil intentions?

Choose **one** image to use as a poster or program cover design for a production of the play. It doesn't matter if you can't draw well. You could use pictures cut from magazines and/or write a paragraph outlining your idea.

When each person has completed this activity, make a display of all the designs. Each 'designer' could then explain the symbolism and intention in his or her design.

Thinking Visually

◆ Evidence ◆

When you look at this ‘spider graph’, you will see that the quotations have been chosen to sum up the feelings of the characters, at various times in the play, towards Macbeth.

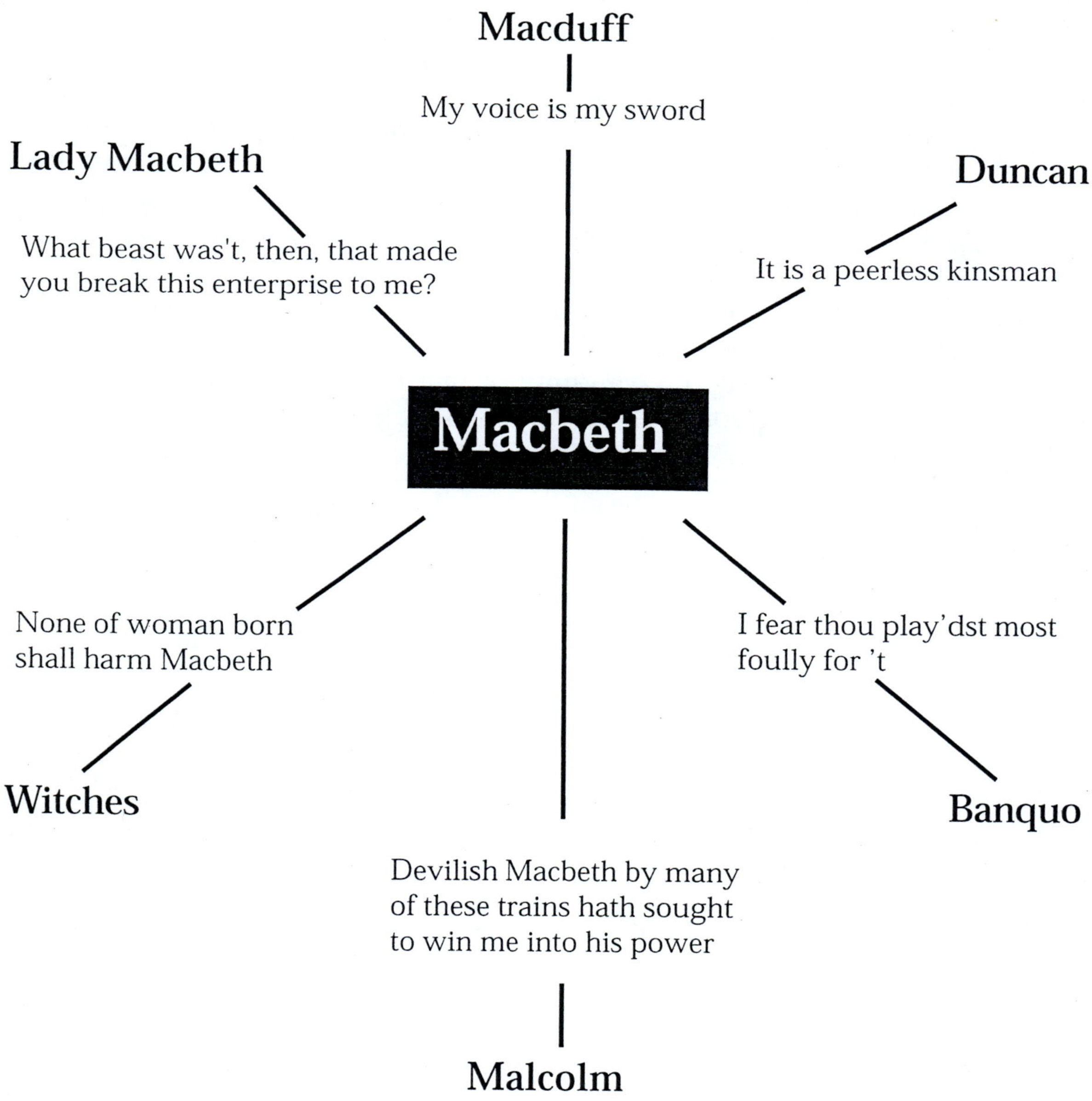

◆ Activity ◆

Would you have chosen the same lines to place around the spider graph? With a partner, discuss the choices in the graph and your alternatives.

Now copy the graph, with arrows reversed. Between you, choose quotations to sum up Macbeth's view of each of the others. Clearly, any single quotation is going to over-simplify Macbeth's feelings, but the discussion and agreement with your partner is the importance of this activity.

Each pair should then copy the final graphs onto large sheets of paper and display them for everyone to compare responses.

◆ Follow up ◆

Diagrams are a valuable aid to memory, as we all tend to remember things more easily that have been presented in a visual way. With your partner, see if you can devise some other ways of showing information about *Macbeth* in diagrammatic form.

For example, you could try a kind of 'path to disaster' for Macbeth, rather like a board game, on which you show the stages of Macbeth's downfall on a winding track.

You might even manage to make this into a 'Snakes and Ladders' cycle of advancement and regression. Or you could make a chart to show the contrasts between Macbeth and Duncan as kings (see activity on Kingship) or plot the rise and fall of Macbeth's and Malcolm's fortunes on a graph.

Question and Answer

◆ Evidence ◆

Questions

1 What does the tyrant?
2 How does my wife?
3 Is't far you ride?
4 Wherefore was that cry?
5 How came she by that light?
6 What is't you do?
7 But who did bid thee join with us?
8 Dismay'd not this our captains, Macbeth and Banquo?
9 What, quite unmann'd in folly?
10 What's to be done?

Answers

a As far, my lord, as will fill up the time twixt this and supper.
b A deed without a name.
c Yes, as sparrows eagles or the hare the lion!
d Why, it stood by her. She has light by her continually.
e If I stand here, I saw him.
f Great Dunsinane he strongly fortifies.
g Be innocent of the knowledge, dearest chuck.
h Why, well.
i The queen, my lord, is dead.
j Macbeth.

◆ Activity ◆

One quotation, either question or answer, is chosen by each student, in such a way that only matching pairs are included. This could be copied on a card or learned. Everyone then walks around the room saying the selected line out loud until the person with the matching half is found. When question and answer are united they sit down and the process continues until no one is left standing. Each pair in turn delivers their question and answer (the rest of the group spots any mistakes) and the whole class tries to identify the context in which these lines are spoken. (Answers are provided at the back of this book as a check on your accuracy.)

◆ Follow up ◆

Props Quiz

This activity helps to recall characters and events.

Each person selects or invents a prop which might be used either by one of the characters in the play at a certain point, or is symbolic of the character in some way. The rest of the group guesses which character it belongs to.

Examples:

Two bloodstained daggers ....Lady Macbeth
A garment too large for him .... Macbeth (see Act 5, scene 2)

Hot Seat

◆ Activity ◆

Working in groups of 6, allocate one of the following characters to each member of the group:

Macbeth, Banquo, Lady Macbeth, Duncan, Macduff, Malcolm

(If numbers don't work out exactly, omit one of the characters or add Lady Macduff.)

Arrange the chairs in a half circle with one chair in front, facing the rest. This is the **hot seat** and when sitting in it you must answer questions **in role** (that is, as the character). The rest of the group are the questioners and are not in role until it is their turn to take the hot seat. Questions which work best are ones about motives and feelings rather than events.

All groups operate simultaneously and move on to a new 'victim' after about five minutes or so. The exact time cannot be set in advance; you have to 'play it by ear', making an on-the-spot judgement about when it seems appropriate to place someone else under interrogation.

Alternative Organisation

Volunteers can take the roles, each with a 'publicity manager' to help field the difficult questions, and the rest of the class become the questioners.

Some sample questions
To Macbeth:
Why did you send a third murderer to join the others?

Of Lady Macbeth:
Why did your relationship with your husband become less intimate after he became king? Did this worry you?

To Macduff:
Why did you leave your wife and family to go to England?

To Duncan:
Why did you learn so little from the experience of Cawdor's treachery?

◆ Follow up ◆

Auditions

Working in pairs, choose any character from the play and select two short 'audition pieces' for the part. Try to find what you feel are the most crucial moments in the play for your selected character. Then join with another pair and audition them both for your part, you trying out **their** pieces. Don't just let them read—try to direct them in the way you feel the lines should be said.

Freeze Frames

◆ Statues ◆

This is a warm-up activity. Work in pairs in a large space. One of you is A, the other B.

1 Person A starts as a sculptor, with person B as the clay to be moulded into a statue of one of the characters in the play at an important moment. Show the rest of the group and let them guess the identity of your statue. Sway over and repeat the process with another statue.

2 Step 2 is to move on to some of the themes and abstract ideas within the play. Try statues of **courage**, then **ambition** and **grief**, showing each one in turn to the class. See if you can suggest other abstract ideas to represent in this symbolic way.

◆ Evidence ◆

1 I have begun to plant thee and will labour to make thee full of growing
(Duncan, Macbeth, Banquo; Act 1, scene 4)

2 O yet I do repent me of my fury that I did kill them.
(Macbeth, Macduff, Banquo, Lady Macbeth and others; Act 2, scene 3)

3 Fail not our feast.
(Macbeth, Lady Macbeth, Banquo; Act 3, scene 1)

4 Which of you hath done this?
(Macbeth, Lady Macbeth, Banquo's ghost, Lords; Act 3, scene 4)

5 What, will the line stretch out to the crack of doom?
((Macbeth, Banquo and descendants, Witches; Act 4, scene 1)

6 Thou liest, thou shag-hair'd villain!
(Lady Macduff, son, murderers; Act 4, scene 2)

7 Out, out damn'd spot, out I say!
(Lady Macbeth, Gentlewoman, Doctor; Act 5, scene 1)

8 If thou speak'st false, upon the next tree shalt thou hang alive.
(Macbeth, Messenger; Act 5, scene 5)

◆ Activity ◆

Each of the lines above represents an important moment in the play. Divide into groups of suitable size and take one of these lines each to present it in a 'freeze frame' or tableau. Try to do more than just show a frozen moment like a still from a film. If you can, show the importance of that particular moment, the relationships of the characters involved and their feelings, by use of body language.

Show your freeze frame to the rest of the class, holding it for a few seconds and asking them to guess who you are and what incident you are presenting, before explaining briefly the effects you were trying to achieve. It isn't the freeze frame itself that is important but the discussion and working out of how to do it.

◆ Follow up ◆

Hamlet, another of Shakespeare's plays, includes a 'play within a play' and it is preceded, as was usually so in Elizabethan drama, by a **dumbshow**. This is a stylised mime which tells the story of the play that is to follow, before any of its lines are spoken. The movements of the dumbshow are exaggerated and symbolic rather than realistic.

Divide into five groups with each group taking one Act of *Macbeth*. The groups work out and present a dumbshow of all the main events of that Act. Don't worry if you haven't enough actors for the parts—double up; be selective, too, about what you choose to show, and keep to the absolute essentials of your Act.

When you have rehearsed, put the five Acts together in order. The presentation of the play in this form also acts as an excellent way of reviewing your understanding of it.

Dreams

◆ Evidence ◆

In Richard's tent. The ghost of Clarence rises.

Ghost *(To King Richard)*
Let me sit heavy on thy soul tomorrow!
I, that was wash'd to death with fulsome wine,
Poor Clarence, by thy guile betray'd to death!
Tomorrow in the battle think on me,
And fall thy edgeless sword: despair, and die!
(To Richmond)
Thou offspring of the house of Lancaster,
The wronged heirs of York do pray for thee:
Good angels guard thy battle! live, and flourish!
(The ghosts of the two young princes rise.)

Ghosts Dream on thy cousins smothr'd in the Tower:
Let us be lead within thy bosom, Richard,
And weigh thee down to ruin, shame and death
Thy nephews' souls bid thee despair and die!
Sleep, Richmond, sleep in peace and wake in joy;
Good angels guard thee from the boar's annoy.
Live, and beget a happy race of kings!
Edward's unhappy sons do bid thee flourish.
(The ghost of Queen Anne rises.)

Ghost Richard, thy wife, that wretched Anne thy wife,
That never slept a quiet hour with thee,
Now fill thy sleep with wretched perturbations:
Tomorrow in the battle think on me.
And fall thy edgeless sword: despair, and die!
(To Richmond)
Thou quiet soul, sleep thou a quiet sleep.
Dream of success and happy victory:
Thy adversary's wide doth pray for thee.
(The ghost of Buckingham rises.)

Ghost *(To King Richard)*
The first was I that help'd thee to the crown;
The last was I that felt thy tyranny:
O, in the battle think on Buckingham,
And die in terror of thy guiltiness!
Dream on, dream on of bloody deeds and death
Fainting, despair; despairing, yield thy breath.
(To Richmond)
I died for hope ere I could lend thee aid:
But cheer thy heart, and be thou not dismayed.
God and good angels fight on Richmond's side
And Richard falls in height of all his pride.
(The ghosts vanish. King Richard wakes out of his dream.)

Richard Give me another horse, —bind my wounds,
Have mercy, Jesu!—Soft! I did but dream.
O coward conscience, how dost thou afflict me
The lights burn blue. —It is now dead midnight.
Cold fearful drops stand on my trembling flesh
My conscience hath a thousand several tongues
And every tongue brings in a several talk
And every tale condemns me for a villain.
I shall despair. There is no creature loves me
And if I die no soul shall pity me:
Nay, wherefore should they, —since that I myself
Find in myself no pity to myself?
Methought the souls of all that I had murdered
Came to my tent; and everyone did threat
Tomorrow's vengeance on the head of Richard.

This is an extract from another play by Shakespeare, *Richard III*, and it is part of a scene, just before Richard's final defeat and death at the Battle of Bosworth, in which his victims appear to him in a dream. (He has been responsible for each of their murders.) Each one in turn curses him and wishes luck the next day to his opponent, Richmond.

Imagine that Macbeth is sleeping before his final battle and that each of **his** victims appears to him in a dream.

Divide into groups of four or five and cast the parts of Macbeth, Banquo, Duncan and Lady Macduff. You can add the Macduff child if you wish, or even Lady Macbeth if you consider her as another of Macbeth's victims. Each person should have a role and will then go off to write a speech—for the victims it will be a speech of accusation; for Macbeth, his reaction to the dream as he wakes in terror at the end. You do not, of course, have to write in blank verse.

Then come back as a group and put the whole thing together. You could add a sleeping Malcolm or Macduff if you like, for the victims to greet with wishes for success in the coming battle.

After some rehearsal, each group could present its scene to the rest of the class.

◆ Follow up ◆

Write your own soliloquy

Choose any moment in the play when we are not given a soliloquy to reveal a character's secret thoughts and feelings and devise your own 'stream of consciousness' for that character at that moment.

Examples:

- Lady Macbeth thinking about Macbeth's behaviour at the banquet.
- Macduff planning revenge on Macbeth for the murder of his family.
- Malcolm as he leaves for England after his father's death.

Remember that a soliloquy always tells the audience the truth as that character sees it.

You could perform your soliloquies for the rest of the class.

Character Jigsaw

◆ Evidence ◆

He that's coming must be provided for. (Act 1, scene 5, ll.65-66)

When you durst do it, then you were a man. (Act 1, scene 3, l.49)

Had he not resembled my father as he slept, I had done't.
(Act 2, scene 2, ll.13-14)

A little water clears us of this deed. (Act 2, scene 2, l.67)

Sit, worthy friends: my lord is often thus,
And hath been from his youth ... (Act 3, scene 4, ll.53-54)

What, will these hands ne'er be clean? (Act 5, scene 1, l.42)

◆ Activity ◆

Each of these six statements by Lady Macbeth represents an aspect of her character. Working with a partner, read them carefully and look at the contexts in which they occur. Discuss which aspects of Lady Macbeth's character you find in each of the statements. Add to the statements any others you would choose to show us Lady Macbeth more clearly, together with anything said about her by others in the play that helps to shed light on her. For example, Duncan calls her an 'honoured hostess', and Macbeth tells her to 'Bring forth men children only'. Remember that the context for each statement is important.

After this, join with another pair and compare your choice of quotations. When you have about 15-20 scraps of text, weave them, in any order, into a composite picture of Lady Macbeth—a sort of 'dramatic collage'. Distribute the lines amongst you (some could be said in chorus, or echoed behind other lines) and use your imaginations to create movements and tableaux to bring out your impressions of her. Rehearse it and present it to the rest of the class.

◆ Follow up ◆

Use the same technique to present a picture of another character of your choice, again using fragments of text to create your jigsaw portrait.

Inquest

◆ Activity ◆

Looking back over the whole play, who do you consider to have been most responsible for Macbeth's downfall? The witches? Lady Macbeth? Macbeth himself? It was clearly a combination of all three, but try to decide who bears the greatest share of blame.

This activity is one way of exploring that question.

First, two or three people act as **Coroners** at an **inquest** on Macbeth — a celestial one so that dead people may give evidence. The purpose of an inquest is to discover the cause or causes of death and to name anyone guilty of bringing it about. The coroners will have the responsibility of making the decisions.

The rest of the class divides into three groups; each group develops a case against **one** of the following: the witches, Lady Macbeth or Macbeth. Choose to do this in any way you like, except that your evidence must not take more than ten minutes to present. You could use characters from the play and ask them to answer questions — in role — put by a Counsel for the Prosecution. Or you could have one person presenting the case and illustrating it by recalling incidents from the play — in freeze frames, mimes or performances of short extracts. Or you could use any combination of these techniques, as well as any ideas of your own. Remember that as you are presenting a case **against** Macbeth, you are to be completely biased, whatever you might really think.

While the three groups are preparing their material, the Coroners arrange the room to look like a court and then draw up a list of questions they wish to ask the possible guilty ones. During the proceedings they are allowed to interrupt to ask any questions they think might help them to reach a just verdict.

When all this preparation is complete (it's probably best to fix a time limit in advance), hold your court and let the Coroners pronounce their findings to the whole class. You will realise that it isn't the verdict that is so important, but the search for evidence and conflicting views.

A Tragic Hero?

◆ Nature of Tragedy ◆

Whatever conclusion you came to in the inquest (previous activity), it is clear that Macbeth bears some responsibility for his downfall. In nearly all of Shakespeare's tragedies, the tragic 'hero' has a mix of good and bad characteristics. The word 'tragedy' is used colloquially today to mean any disaster, but in the theatre it has a more specialised meaning. If you have ever seen a Shakespearean tragedy in the theatre, you will probably have experienced this special phenomenon: the audience feels some empathy and sympathy with the hero, however wicked his deeds, yet also experiences a sense of justice in his downfall.

In ancient Greece, Aristotle, trying to analyse this special experience in the theatre, concluded that the tragic hero must be neither wholly good (or his fate will be **too** painful for the audience), nor wholly bad (or there will not be that essential element of sympathy for a fellow human being).

How do you think these ideas might apply to *Macbeth*? Do we at least start with some sympathy for him? If so, how does Shakespeare make us feel this?

◆ Activity ◆

With a partner, discuss this question and draw up a list of points about what we can find that to some extent excuses Macbeth, such as his physical courage, the witches' influence, and his lyrical language, which seems to reveal an essentially noble mind. Then draw up a similar list of how we come to see his death at the hands of Macduff as just and right.

Bring these notes to a full class discussion on the truth or otherwise of Malcolm's verdict on the Macbeths:

> … this dead butcher and his fiend-like queen

◆ Follow up ◆

Write an essay about your final view of Macbeth. Devise your own essay title so that you can argue strongly for your own point of view. Remember that your arguments should be related to particular events and speeches of the play.

Answers to Question and Answer Game
(Activity 15, page 29)

1 (f) Malcolm's army approaching Dunsinane (Act 5, scene 2)

2 (h) Macduff in England asking about his family (Act 4, scene 3)

3 (a) Macbeth asking Banquo about his plans (Act 3, scene 1)

4 (i) Macbeth hears of Lady Macbeth's death (Act 5, scene 5)

5 (d) Doctor questions Gentlewoman about Lady Macbeth's sleepwalking (Act 5, scene 1)

6 (b) Macbeth consulting witches (Act 4, scene 1)

7 (j) Murder of Banquo — Third Murderer (Act 3, scene 3)

8 (c) Duncan questions captain about the battle (Act 1, scene 2)

9 (e) Lady Macbeth reproaches Macbeth for his reaction to Banquo's ghost (Act 3, scene 3)

10 (g) Macbeth and Lady Macbeth speaking of Banquo's murder (Act 3, scene 2)

Shakespeare on Stage: Drama Techniques

This chapter draws attention to aspects of Shakespeare's plays as performed theatrical works. It will look beyond a mere analysis of the words in the script and will focus on those techniques relevant to the play as a staged performance.

In recent years emphasis has been placed on plays as performance pieces and for many students and teachers this has caused some difficulties. It is acknowledged that the field, especially the discipline of performance semiotics, is problematic for teachers and students alike:

> *Learning how to interpret and analyse theatrical events is a critical component in the education of students... However, there is very little available to guide teachers who are struggling...How are teachers supposed to help students become more responsive to theatrical events? What skills do students need in order to openly receive and actively interpret a variety of performance texts?* (Grady, 2000, p144).

This chapter provides guidelines for analysing a Shakespeare play as a live, theatrical event.

◆ Performance Semiotics ◆

Drama examination questions for senior students now demand an understanding of performance semiotics, that is, the signs which convey meaning from the stage to the audience, and the dynamic between the actors and the audience. Where once, in examination questions, there was a concentration on issues such as characters and themes, students are now faced with more complex areas to comment on.

For example in 2001 the following questions appeared in the English paper for the New South Wales Higher School Certificate:

2/3 Unit Common English, Paper II.
Question 3 (Drama):
In what ways do playwrights use dramatic techniques to present their ideas in the two plays you have studied from the list below?
Arthur Miller: *The Crucible*
William Shakespeare: *Macbeth*
Sophocles: *Antigone*
Katherine Thomson: *Diving for Pearls.*

English Advanced, Section II
Question 4:
How might different productions dramatise the struggle between chaos and order in *King Lear*?

◆ Dramatic Techniques ◆

English teachers and their students are familiar with those elements of drama criticism which also apply to literary analysis. We refer here to the story, the structure of the work, characters, themes, motives, language, imagery, symbols, genre, socio-political context, historical context, gender issues and ideological positions. These areas are well covered when studying either a novel or a play. This chapter does not concentrate on these issues because most teachers and students are familiar with them. It needs to be stressed, however that the above aspects are also part of the dramatic devices of a play.

◆ Script and Performance ◆

One of the major developments in recent performance studies research is the way in which readers of scripts have begun to focus on the fact that play scripts are written to be performed and a critical response to a play must reflect the fact that the script is a blueprint for a live happening. The realisation of such an event will require the creative input of a range of talents. The performing arts involve enactments which bond audiences and performers in a shared set of experiences to which both make differing contributions; hence each performance of the same written text is unique (Hughes, J, 1998). The dynamics of actor and actor, actor and director, actor and audience, change with every enactment. It follows that students must study a play both in the theatre and as text, and that our study of text must all the time take account of what could be happening on stage. (Carlson, M, 1996)

However, there are students who write about a play, in examinations, as if the play were a novel. It is not uncommon to read papers in which students write "In the novel *Hamlet*, Shakespeare tells us about...". This confusion is not entirely unjustified because if one looks at the types of critical concerns teachers and students have traditionally applied to drama the following appear: themes, plot, character, structure, symbols, imagery and tone, and the like. In order to study a play as a performed work, students need to explore the fact that a play script is a springboard for collaborative action.

Unlike poetry or the novel, there is no intimate relationship implicit between the reader and a play script. A play script is written for a team – directors, designers, actors etc. – to bring to life. It is not possible to read a text for performance without responding to the different genre within the script. For example, at one point the reader will need to interpret as an actor, at another as a designer. Critical sensibilities and comprehension strategies must be developed which allow the reader 'to recognise that the play script consists of a set of instructions to actors, directors, designers and technicians' (Michaels, W, 1991).

This chapter looks at drama elements which particularly relate to plays as performance pieces. These are: plot, plot points, and plot and character, the theatre performance space, setting, lighting, focus, music and sound effects, props and costumes, actors, proxemics, pace and tempo changes.

◆ The Plot ◆

When reading a script, or seeing a play, it is important to draw a distinction between the sections of the plot that occur on stage and the story that we learn about. This is a useful distinction when exploring drama techniques because it draws our attention to the decisions a playwright has made concerning what will be highlighted on stage. Information that is presented though actions and words, on stage, is likely to have more impact on an audience's focus than information which is reported.

In terms of drama techniques, it is interesting to explore the parts of the plot Shakespeare decides will happen on stage and what we will simply be told about. For example, we learn, in *Othello*, that Othello and Desdemona are married. This is part of the story, but not part of the staged plot. The play is focussing on the events after Othello and Desdemona's marriage, not on their wedding per se. In *Antony and Cleopatra*, we do not see a coronation of Cleopatra because it's not central to the action of her relationship with Antony. We know she is Queen, that is part of the story, but how she got there is not a major part of the staged plot of *Antony and Cleopatra*.

◆ Plot Points ◆

A play, or any dramatic work of art, has a plot structure: the twists and turns that keep our interest and tell the story. Each point in the story, where the plot turns on its journey, can be called a **plot point**: the arrival of a character, the exposing of a secret, a discovery. The first plot point is when the audience realises what is at stake or what type of story this is going to be. For example, in *Romeo and Juliet* it is when the two teenagers meet. We already know the families are sworn enemies so a possible romance between the two teenagers signals the conflict and the drama ahead.

◆ Plot and Character ◆

The plot, in many of Shakespeare's plays, is often tied very closely to the actions of one or more characters. For example Macbeth plots his way to the throne; Romeo and Juliet have their separate plots that meet and destroy them both.

Teachers and students studying a Shakespeare play should fill out a basic play grid for each scene of the play in order to visualise what is happening on stage and follow the plot. The play grid should show: the setting, who enters, who exits and what happens.

◆ Theatre Performance Space ◆

The performance space is a major part of the dramatic techniques employed by a playwright. The space in which a play is performed conveys many drama messages. We have a very different expectation when we view a performance at an opera house from than we have when we view a performance by a travelling circus. When studying Shakespeare's plays, we have to envisage the Elizabethan performance space, such as the Globe Theatre, and what this would have meant for the audience.

The Globe was situated across the River Thames in the seediest part of town, amidst the other forms of 'low' entertainment such as brothels, bear baiting and cock fighting. People did not go along expecting a high- brow, cultured event (Gurr, A, 1987). They would wander in and out of the performances, eat and drink and have assignations. As a consequence, Shakespeare's plays have much repetition in them so that if you missed part of the plot the first time, you understood it the second time.

This is very different from the traditional theatre space that we are used to today. Now, the audience generally faces the stage, sits in the dark and fully concentrates on the play. Hence, in contemporary performances of Shakespeare's plays, much of the text is often deleted because we experience a very different theatre world, one where messages are sent and received in a more concentrated time and space frame.

◆ Viewing the Stage ◆

At the Globe Theatre, in Shakespeare's day, the audience sat or stood on three sides of the thrust stage. This meant that they interacted with each other and became part of the visual picture of the performance. The actors were performing to three sides and competing for the audience's attention. As the plays took place in daylight, the audience was as visible as were the actors. Some people could see very little of the performers. For instance,there was limited seating above the stage on the first balcony, known as the Lords' Boxes. Here the aristocracy or wealthy merchants would sit here so as to be seen by the masses.

◆ The Fictional Space of the Stage ◆

Unlike many of today's stages, the Globe used extremely limited set pieces, meaning that any indication of setting for scenes was conveyed principally through the language of the play. The fictional space of the performance changed rapidly and this is made plausible by the 'wipe and clear' method of staging, by which actors' entrances establish a new fictional space for each scene.

If the scene were to alter, for example in Othello , from a dark night street scene to a raging storm, the actors would have to establish this with the audience through their language. For example see how the scene is set in these words:

Act II, scene I

Montano: *What from the cape do you discern at sea?*

First Gent: *Nothing at all, it is a high-wrought flood.*
I cannot 'twixt the heaven and the main
Descry a sail.

Montano: *Methinks the wind hath spoke aloud at land;*
A fuller blast ne'er shook our battlements.
If it hath ruffianed so upon the sea,
What ribs of oak, when mountains melt on them,
Can hold the mortise? What shall we hear of this?

◆ The Stage Picture ◆

We know that Shakespeare did not write many explicit stage directions in his texts, yet settings, stage movements and actions are often embedded in the text (Styan, 1977).

◆ The Setting ◆

As we can see from above example from *Othello,* the setting in Shakespeare's plays is established by the words the actors speak; it is embedded in the text.

The setting is a major dramatic technique and conveys meaning. Indoor settings are often associated with more intimate relationships between the characters. For example, much of Macbeth is set indoors as the dark intrigues and murderous plots of *Macbeth* and Lady Macbeth unfold. These deeds eventually turn in upon themselves and destroy the Macbeths.

King Lear, on the other hand, is very much an outdoor play, and the huge themes encompassed in this play are reinforced by the wild elements to which its characters are exposed. As the personal tragedy of Lear unfolds and his alienation from those he loves becomes more extreme, the setting shifts increasingly towards the hostile, natural world. Note how the wildness of the setting is established in Lear's words:

King Lear, Act III, scene I

Lear: *"Blow, winds, and crack your cheeks. Rage, blow.*
You cataracts and hurricanoes, spout
Till you have drenched our steeples, drowned the cocks.
You sulph'rous and thought executing fires,
Vaunt-couriers to oak-cleaving thunderbolts,
Singe my white head. And thou, all-shaking thunder,
Strike flat the thick rotundity o' th' world,
Crack Nature's moulds, all germains spill at once,
That makes ingrateful man".

Kenneth Tynan, in his 1992 review of Peter Brooke's King Lear, wrote that the stage is "empty and sterile, a bare space of hostile earth".

You will find another well established and important setting in *Richard II* in Act III, scene iv.

Queen *What sport shall we devise here in this garden,*
To drive away the heavy thought of care?

[First] Lady *Madam, we'll play at bowls.*

Queen *'Twill make me think the world is full of rubs,*
And that my fortune runs against the bias.

[Second] Lady *Madam, we'll dance.*

Queen *My legs can keep no measure in delight*
When my poor heart no measure keeps in grief;
Therefore no dancing, girl. Some other sport.

[First] Lady *Madam, we'll tell tales.*

Queen *Of sorrow or of joy?*

[First] Lady *Of Either, madam.*

Queen *Of neither, girl.*
For if of joy, being altogether wanting,
It doth remember me the more of sorrow.
Or if of grief, being altogether had,
It adds more sorrow to my want of joy.
For what I have I need not to repeat,
And what I want it boots not to complain.

[Second] Lady *Madam, I'll sing.*

Many critics see the garden as a significant metaphor for the themes in *Richard II*. Here we see another example of the setting forming part of the dramatic techniques of a Shakespeare play.

◆ Performances Today ◆

Nowadays a crucial factor in a performance of Shakespeare is that the setting can be established by scenery or in the cinema by the location. This can mean that the words used by Elizabethan actors to establish the setting verbally may be redundant in such performances.

◆ Stage Directions ◆

As noted above, Shakespeare did not write many explicit stage directions in his texts, yet, just as with settings, stage movements and actions are often embedded in the texts . In this section, we will looking at some of those embedded directions.

◆ Lighting ◆

Lighting can be used to evoke setting and mood and will change the appearance of a stage. In today's theatre the lighting will, for example, signify to us whether it is day or night. As we have already seen, Shakespeare's plays were performed in daylight and so if it is a night-time setting, the actor's words will need to tell us.

Macbeth is a very dark play and many of the scenes occur at night. For example, in Act 5 scene I, to establish the night setting for Lady Macbeth's sleep walking scene the Doctor says to the Gentlewomen:

'I have two nights watched with you…'

and as Lady Macbeth enters he says:

'How came she by that light?'.
So we know it is night!

Shakespeare himself sends up this need in one of Bottom's speeches from *A Midsummer Night's Dream*. Bottom, as we know, is a very poor actor, but he wants to make sure that the members of Theseus' court, who are watching the play, know that it is taking place at night.

A Midsummer Night's Dream, Act IV, sc.ii.

Bottom (as Pyramus)
O grim-looked night, O night with hue so black,
O night which ever art when day is not;
O night, O night, alack, alack, alack.

Lighting can also be used to draw focus to one space or character on stage. In Shakespeare's day, however, that dramatic device was not available, and so he would use other dramatic devices, such as movement, to draw focus to a character.

◆ Focus ◆

A skilled playwright can make sure that we focus on a particular character (or set of characters) in a scene so that we pay attention to their actions even though actions and words of other characters may be happening at the same time.

For example, in *Hamlet*, Act I, scene ii, there is a large cast on stage: Claudius, Gertrude, Councillors, Polonius, Laertes, Hamlet and many others, including Voltemand and Cornelius. And yet, our focus is on Hamlet. What is the dramatic technique that Shakespeare uses to make us focus on Hamlet? The court is very busy, with Claudius making large diplomatic speeches and various members of the Court making public speeches. Hamlet, we learn, is dressed in black and taking no part in the direct action except to make asides. He appears gloomy, and we learn this from Claudius' words:

" How is it that the clouds still hang on you?"

In the midst of all this action, a character standing away from the action and juxtaposed to the action will still gain our focus even though he has little to say and moves very little. Shakespeare's isolation of Hamlet is a dramatic technique that focuses the audience on Hamlet.

An actor does not need to have lines to say in order to draw focus on stage. Another way to gain focus is for an actor to move. In Act V, scene ii of Hamlet, much is happening. Laertes and Hamlet are fighting and Claudius is seeking to hide his treachery. Look at the following exchange:

King Claudius	*Part them, they are incensed.*
Hamlet	*Nay, come again.*
Osric	*Look to the Queen there, ho!*
Horatio	*They bleed on both sides.* *How is 't, my lord?*
Osric	*How is 't, Laertes?*
Laertes	*Why, as a woodcock to mine own springe, Osric.* *I am justly killed with mine own treachery.*
Hamlet	*How does the Queen?*
King Claudius	*She swoons to see them bleed.*

We learn from these lines that the Queen has fainted. In the act of her falling down on stage, all focus would go to the Queen. This is a dramatic technique used by Shakespeare to draw attention to the Queen even though she has no lines to say at this point.

In today's theatre, focus is often given to a character by use of lighting. A spotlight on the Queen at this point in the play would also increase the audience's attention on her.

◆ Music and Sound ◆

Music can have several effects. It evokes mood, it can set the scene and often leads the audience to predict certain actions.

Music can be used before any text is spoken to set the scene. Ken Watson, the commissioning editor of St Clair Press, recalls a noteworthy production of *Twelfth Night* by the Royal Shakespeare Company where this was done. As the audience entered the theatre a group of musicians were playing tavern-like music. This changed to courtly music and then the Duke entered. He mimed courtly activities (reading submissions, sealing documents etc) with his courtiers. Only then when the scene was set did he say the opening lines.

Duke	*If music be the food of love, play on;*

◆ Songs and Dances ◆

There are many other examples of the use of music in Shakespeare's plays. Many of the plays feature songs and descriptions of dances. Characters often use songs to give insight into their emotional state at a given time, for example, Desdemona's "Willow song" in Othello. From Act IV, scene iii:

Desdemona

My mother had a maid called Barbary.
She was in love, and he she loved proved mad
And did forsake her. She had a song of willow.
An old thing 'twas, but it expressed her fortune,
And she died singing it. That song tonight
Will not go from my mind. I have much to do
But to go hang my head all at one side
And sing it, like poor Barbary. Prithee, dispatch.

Emilia

Shall I go fetch your nightgown?

Desdemona

No. Unpin me here.
This Lodovico is a proper man.

Emilia

A very handsome man.

Desdemona

He speaks well.

Emilia

I know a lady in Venice would have walked
barefoot to Palestine for a touch of his nether lip.

Desdemona

"The poor soul sat sighing by a sycamore tree,
Sing all a green willow.
Her hand on her bosom, her head on her knee,
The fresh streams ran by her and murmured her moans,
Sing willow, willow, willow.
Her salt tears fell from her and softened the stones,
Sing willow"-
Lay by these.-"willow, willow."
Prithee, hie thee. He'll come anon.
"Sing all a green willow must be my garland.
"Let nobody blame him, his scorn approve"-
Nay, that's not next. Hark, who is 't that knocks?

Emilia

It's the wind.

The song is a dramatic technique which displays Desdemona's feelings of desolation and sadness.

Songs can also be humorous, and act to provide a light-hearted break from the emotional gravity of surrounding scenes. This is well illustrated by the Gravediggers' song from Act V, scene i in Hamlet. The content is humorous but also underlines the tragedy of Ophelia's death and abandonment by Hamlet.

First Clown	*Cudgel thy brains no more about it, for your dull ass will not mend his pace with beating; and when you are asked this question next, say "a grave-maker"; the houses that he makes lasts till doomsday. Go, get thee to Johan. Fetch me a stoup of liquor.* *In youth when I did love, did love, Methought it was very sweet To contract-O-the time for-a-my behove, O methought there-a-was nothing-a-meet.*
Hamlet	*Has this fellow no feeling of his business that a sings at grave-making?*
Horatio	*Custom hath made it in him a property of easiness.*
Hamlet	*'Tis e'en so; the hand of little employment hath the daintier sense.*
First Clown	*But age with his stealing steps Hath caught me in his clutch, And hath shipped me intil the land, As if I had never been such.*

There are also examples in the Shakespearian text where actors indicate that musical instruments such as trumpets were included in Elizabethan performances. These sounds often herald the entrance of significant characters. The following example is taken from *Richard II*, Act I, scene iii.

Lord Marshal	*My lord Aumerle, is Harry Hereford armed?*
Aumerle	*Yea, at all points, and longs to enter in.*
Lord Marshal	*The Duke of Norfolk, sprightfully and bold, Stays but the summons of the appellant's trumpet.*
Aumerle	*Why then, the champions are prepared, and stay For nothing but his majesty's approach.*

◆ Sound Effects ◆

We know that sound effects were also used in Elizabethan Theatre. There is evidence to suggest that barrels were rolled across the floor of the roof cavity above the stage to give the effect of thunder. An associated effect, the firing of a projectile, led to the destruction of the first Globe theatre in a performance of *Henry VIII* when the roof thatching caught fire and spread to the rest of the theatre.

◆ Props and Costumes ◆

Props and costumes are elements of the staged drama which, depending on their type, function and relationship to the space and actors' bodies, convey meaning to audiences (Pavis,1985: 209).

Props are anything that can be carried on stage; for example a sword, a candle, a goblet. They may or may not be used by characters, but are usually incorporated because they somehow change the workings of the play. For example, the handkerchief in *Othello*, the dagger in *Macbeth* and Ophelia's flowers in *Hamlet* are dramatic uses of props.

Props often become associated with a character and can be used to enhance that character when they are present or absent. For example, the wearing of a crown carries symbolic dramatic meaning, that is, the person is a king or queen.

◆ Costumes ◆

Costuming is an important aspect of live theatre performance. Costumes identify characters as belonging to social groups by providing such information as their social status, wealth and occupation. The colours and styles of costuming may also convey dramatic meaning by having symbolic significance. In Elizabethan times, a person's status and rank was determined by the costumes they wore. The Elizabethan costumes were elaborate, but familiar to Elizabethan audiences. They would know from the costume the status of a character as these social systems applied to themselves. Actors were considered scandalous as they dressed as royalty or as women.

◆ Actors ◆

When looking at dramatic techniques we cannot forget the casting of the actors and their style of performing (Pavis, 1985:210). The actors in Elizabethan performances were always male, with young pre-pubescent boys often playing the parts of women. This becomes especially significant when examining the way that audiences would have related to the tone of scenes. Whereas today's audiences would view scenes from *Romeo and Juliet* as romantic and weighty, perhaps Elizabethan audiences would have found the image of two men acting the part of male and female lovers hilarious.

Scenes in which Shakespeare describes the differences between men and women would also have been humorous to Elizabethan audiences given the cross-gendered casting that occurred. A good example is the Nurse's description of Romeo in Act II, scene v:

Nurse *Well, you have made a simple choice. You know not how to choose a man.*

Romeo? *No, not he; though his face be better than any man's, yet his leg excels all*
men's, and for a hand and a foot and a body, though
they be not to be talked on, yet they are past compare.
He is not the flower of courtesy, but,
I'll warrant him, as gentle as a lamb. Go thy ways, wench. Serve God.
What, have you dined at home?

This is a very risque speech and, no doubt, the Elizabethan audience would have derived much humorous pleasure from it, especially as it is delivered by a male dressed up as a female.

◆ Actors' Status ◆

In Elizabethan days, actors were not considered as high-status professionals and often held other trades. In today's productions or films, the opposite is true. Consequently, today's audiences are far more likely to accept a relationship of separation between audience/actor than in Elizabethan performances. Familiarity, or lack of familiarity, with the real persona of an actor affects the way that audiences view a performance and place themselves within it.

In today's theatre and film, well-known actors come with what is called a tag. That is, the character traits developed from their previous performances. In the Mel Gibson film of Hamlet, we cannot completely divorce Hamlet from Mel Gibson's previous roles such as in Lethal Weapon. In terms of our reception of a performance, Hamlet played by Mel Gibson is a man of action. Kenneth Branagh's Hamlet does not carry this tag.

◆ Proxemics ◆

Vitally important… is everything to do with the performers' occupation of the space, their entrances, exits, other movements and gestures and the proxemic relationships that these moves and gestures set up between actors, spectators, objects and the space itself. These movements and the groupings become meaningful only when situated in the given space and they are the major means whereby that space is activated and itself made meaningful. (McAuley, G, 2000: 8)

Shakespeare often uses spatial relationships between actors to create dramatic effects. If we look for example at the opening of Hamlet, we see Bernardo and Francisco moving quickly across the stage at midnight, setting the scene. Horatio and Marcellus enter and move about a lot, indicating that something strange is going on. The Ghost enters and is established as separate from the group. The stage proxemics establish a scene of tension and fear. We know that something perilous is happening.

Proxemics are often used to create great tension on stage. In 1989, the following question appeared in the New South Wales Higher School Certificate English examination paper:

Question 3: Read the following extract from Othello carefully.

What does the passage illustrate about the dramatic qualities and the concerns of the play?

Othello *It is the cause, it is the cause, my soul.*
Let me not name it to you, you chaste stars.
It is the cause. Yet I'll not shed her blood,
Nor scar that whiter skin of hers than snow,
And smooth as monumental alabaster.
Yet she must die, else she'll betray more men.
Put out the light, and then put out the light.
If I quench thee, thou flaming minister,
I can again thy former light restore
Should I repent me; but once put out thy light,
Thou cunning'st pattern of excelling nature,
I know not where is that Promethean heat
That can thy light relume. When I have plucked thy rose
I cannot give it vital growth again.
It needs must wither. I'll smell thee on the tree.

O balmy breath, that dost almost persuade
Justice to break her sword! One more, one more.
Be thus when thou art dead, and I will kill thee
And love thee after. One more, and that's the last.

So sweet was ne'er so fatal. I must weep,
But they are cruel tears. This sorrow's heavenly,
It strikes where it doth love. She wakes.

Desdemona *Who's there? Othello?*

Othello *Ay, Desdemona.*

Desdemona *Will you come to bed, my lord?*

Othello *Have you prayed tonight, Desdemon?*

Desdemona *Ay, my lord.*

Othello *If you bethink yourself of any crime*
Unreconciled as yet to heaven and grace,
Solicit for it straight.

Desdemona *Alack, my lord, what may you mean by that?*

Othello *Well, do it, and be brief. I will walk by.*
I would not kill thy unpreparèd spirit.
No, heavens forfend! I would not kill thy soul.

Desdemona *Talk you of killing?*

Othello *Ay, I do.*

Desdemona *Then heaven*
Have mercy on me.

Othello *Amen, with all my heart.*

This question, asking about dramatic qualities, caused many students and teachers great concerns as they didn't know what this meant. To answer this question, we need to visualise the stage picture. Desdemona is asleep in her bed downstage toward the audience. Othello enters from the back and slowly walks towards her from "It is the cause" to "I'll smell thee on the tree". Given the amount of words he has to speak here, it must be a very slow walk. When a character, that is intent on murder, moves very slowly to his victim, it creates almost unbearable tension in the viewer. We only have to think of those slow movements in Hitchcock, and other horror films, where tension and suspense is built by the slow movements of the camera. In answering this question on *Othello*, one of the key issues the students needed to note is the proxemic relationship between the two actors and how Othello's action of moving slowly toward Desdemona is a dramatic technique designed to charge the audience with anxiety.

◆ Pace and Tempo Changes ◆

A play is a performance piece. If we were studying music, it would be inconceivable not to analyse pace and tempo changes. In the great symphonies of Mozart and Beethoven, there are slow movements and quick movements (largo and allegro). Plays are also performance pieces and so good playwrights, such as Shakespeare, make sure there are tempo changes. A play that moves at exactly the same tempo throughout the entire performance becomes very monotonous and boring for an audience.

In Shakespeare, we often find slow movements followed by very fast movements and this is a dramatic device. The following examples give some idea as to how these changes in pace/tempo take place.

An example of this dramatic technique can be found in *Hamlet*, Act III, scene iii and Act III, scene iv. In Act III, scene iii, Hamlet has a long speech in which he contemplates killing Claudius.

Hamlet *Now might I do it pat, now he is praying,*
And now I'll do 't,
and so he goes to heaven,
And so am I revenged. That would be scanned.
A villain kills my father, and for that
I, his sole son, do this same villain send
To heaven.
O, this is hire and salary, not revenge!
He took my father grossly, full of bread,
With all his crimes broad blown, as flush as May;
And how his audit stands, who knows save heaven?
But in our circumstance and course of thought
'Tis heavy with him. And am I then revenged
To take him in the purging of his soul,
When he is fit and seasoned for his passage?
Number
Up, sword, and know thou a more horrid hint.
When he is drunk asleep, or in his rage,
Or in th' incestuous pleasure of his bed,
At gaming, swearing, or about some act |
That has no relish of salvation in 't,
Then trip him that his heels may kick at heaven,
And that his soul may be as damned and black
As hell whereto it goes. My mother stays.
This physic but prolongs thy sickly days.

The tempo of this long speech juxtaposes with the tempo of the short, sharp lines that follow between Hamlet and his mother in the next scene:

Hamlet	*Now, mother, what's the matter?*
Queen	*Hamlet, thou hast thy father much offended.*
Hamlet	*Mother, you have my father much offended.*
Queen	*Come, come, you answer with an idle tongue.*
Hamlet	*Go, go, you question with a wicked tongue.*
Queen	*Why, how now, Hamlet?*

In order to change the tempo, Shakespeare will often juxtapose a very grave and grim scene with a humorous scene.

Macbeth, Act II, scene ii, is a very serious and intimate scene in which Macbeth and Lady Macbeth discuss the killing of Duncan. It is immediately followed by a riotous and robust scene by the Porter. This juxtaposition not only changes the pace but would give the groundlings entertainment.

In the concluding scenes of the *Macbeth*, Shakespeare builds the tension by placing a number of short but extremely active scenes together. These scenes depict the warring of Macbeth and Macduff's respective factions. By placing a series of short, fast scenes together where actors are walking on and off in a nearly continuous stream, Shakespeare builds the pace and tension. The pace and tension is interrupted by the scene in which Lady Macbeth's death is reported. These shifts in pace and tempo draw the audience into the action of the play and direct the audience's attention to various characters or occurrences.

When studying a Shakespearian play, one should look for Shakespeare's use of the dramatic technique of tempo and pace changes.

◆ Conclusion ◆

The great drama educator, Dorothy Heathcote (1979), stated that a theatrical performance consisted of only six basic elements:

Sound	Silence
Movement	Stillness
Lightness	Darkness

She challenged us to find anything more. It is arguable that there is more. However, she has highlighted that plays are living performance pieces and that we must analyse the dramatic techniques and activities that are happening on stage. As Grotowski, the famous twentieth century director stated "...the theatre is an act carried out **here** and **now** in the actors' organisms, in front of other men (sic)" (1969: 119).

When studying a Shakespeare text, we need to visualise the performance as taking place within a defined space. Further, we must visualise how an audience would be reacting and responding to this.

Drama techniques consist of the conventional aspects: characters, structure, themes, language, socio-political context etc. However, for a full understanding of drama techniques used in Shakespeare's plays we need to address the stage picture: theatre space, the theatre performance space, setting, lighting, focus, music and sound effects, props and costumes, actors, proxemics, pace and tempo changes.

Students should approach the study of a Shakespearian play as if they were going to direct a performance. They should ask themselves at all times the following questions:

- What is the performance space?
- What is the relationship between stage and audience?
- What is the setting?
- What time of day is it?
- Who enters?
- What do they say?
- What do they do?
- Who has the focus?
- Where are characters in relationship to others on stage?
- What are they wearing?
- What props do they use?
- What is the tempo of the scene?
- When do characters exit?

The answer to these questions, together with the more familiar literary criticism issues (language, themes etc), will develop an understanding of the drama techniques employed by the playwright.

References

Carlson, M, 1996, *Performance: a critical introduction*, London: Routledge.

Grady, S, 2000, 'Languages of the stage: a critical framework for analysing and creating performance' in H Nicolson, (ed), *Teaching Drama 11-18*, London: Continuum.

Grotowski, J, 1969, *Towards a Poor Theatre*, London: Methuen.

Gurr, Andrew, 1987, *Playgoing in Shakespeare's London*, Cambridge University Press.

Heathcote, Dorothy, 1979, *Three Looms Waiting*, (Video Cassette), BBC Omnibus.

Hughes, J, (1998), 'Teaching Plays As Theatre', In W Sawyer, K Watson and E Gold (eds), *Re-viewing English* (pp 277-285), Sydney: St Clair Press.

McAuley, Gay, 2000, *Space In Performance, Making Meaning In Theatre*, University of Michigan Press.

Michaels, W, 1991, 'Teaching Texts' in Hughes, J (ed), 1991 *Drama in Education: The State of the Art*, Education Drama Association New South Wales.

Pavis, Patrice, 1985, 'Theatre Analysis: Some Questions And A Questionaire' *New Theatre Quarterly*, Vol 1 (2) May, pp 208-212.

Styan, J L, 1977, *Shakespeare's Stagecraft*, Cambridge University Press.

Tynan, K, 1962, 'King Lear', Review. *The Observer*, November.